50 Quick Ways to go from Good to Outstanding

By Mike Gershon

Text Copyright © 2016 Mike Gershon

All Rights Reserved

About the Author

Mike Gershon is known in the United Kingdom and beyond as an expert educationalist whose knowledge of teaching and learning is rooted in classroom practice. His online teaching tools have been viewed and downloaded more than 3.5 million times, making them some of the most popular of all time.

He is the author of over 80 books and guides covering different areas of teaching and learning. Some of Mike's bestsellers include books on assessment for learning, questioning, differentiation and outstanding teaching, as well as Growth Mindsets. You can train online with Mike, from anywhere in the world, at www.tes.com/institute/cpd-courses-teachers.

You can also find out more at www.mikegershon.com and www.gershongrowthmindsets.com, including about Mike's inspirational in-school training and student workshops.

Training and Consultancy

Mike offers a range of training and consultancy services covering all areas of teaching and learning, raising achievement and classroom practice. Examples of recent training events include:

- Assessment for Learning: Theory and Practice Keynote Address – Leigh Academies Trust Conference, London
- Growth Mindsets: Staff Training, Student Workshops and Speech to Parents – Longton Primary School, Preston
- Effective Questioning to Raise Achievement – Shireland Collegiate Academy, Birmingham

To find out more, visit www.mikegershon.com or www.gershongrowthmindsets.com or get in touch via mike@mikegershon.com

Other Works from the Same Author

Available to buy now on Amazon:

How to use Differentiation in the Classroom: The Complete Guide

How to use Assessment for Learning in the Classroom: The Complete Guide

How to use Bloom's Taxonomy in the Classroom: The Complete Guide

How to use Questioning in the Classroom: The Complete Guide

How to use Discussion in the Classroom: The Complete Guide

How to Manage Behaviour in the Classroom: The Complete Guide

How to Teach EAL Students in the Classroom: The Complete Guide

How to be an Outstanding Trainee Teacher: The Complete Guide

More Secondary Starters and Plenaries

Secondary Starters and Plenaries: History

Teach Now! History: Becoming a Great History Teacher

The Growth Mindset Pocketbook (with Professor Barry Hymer)

The Exams, Tests and Revision Pocketbook (from April 2016)

Also available to buy now on Amazon, the entire 'Quick 50' Series:

50 Quick and Brilliant Teaching Ideas

50 Quick and Brilliant Teaching Techniques

50 Quick and Easy Lesson Activities

50 Quick Ways to Help Your Students Secure A and B Grades at GCSE

50 Quick Ways to Help Your Students Think, Learn, and Use Their Brains Brilliantly

50 Quick Ways to Motivate and Engage Your Students

50 Quick Ways to Outstanding Teaching

50 Quick Ways to Perfect Behaviour Management

50 Quick and Brilliant Teaching Games

50 Quick and Easy Ways Leaders Can Prepare for Ofsted

50 Quick and Easy Ways to Outstanding Group Work

50 Quick and Easy Ways to Prepare for Ofsted

50 Quick Ways to Stretch and Challenge More-Able Students

50 Quick Ways to Create Independent Learners

50 Quick Ways to go from Good to Outstanding

50 Quick Ways to Support Less-Able Learners

And forthcoming in Summer 2016:

50 Quick Ways to Get Past 'I Don't Know'

50 Quick Ways to Start Your Lesson with a Bang!

50 Quick Ways to Improve Literacy Across the Curriculum

50 Quick Ways to Success with Life After Levels

50 Quick Ways to Improve Feedback and Marking

50 Quick and Brilliant Teaching Games – Part Two

50 Quick Ways to Use Scaffolding and Modelling

50 Quick Ways to a Better Work-Life Balance

About the Series

The 'Quick 50' series was born out of a desire to provide teachers with practical, tried and tested ideas, activities, strategies and techniques which would help them to teach brilliant lessons, raise achievement and engage and inspire their students.

Every title in the series distils great teaching wisdom into fifty bite-sized chunks. These are easy to digest and easy to apply – perfect for the busy teacher who wants to develop their practice and support their students.

Acknowledgements

My thanks to all the staff and students I have worked with past and present, particularly those at Pimlico Academy and King Edward VI School, Bury St Edmunds. Thanks also to the teachers and teaching assistants who have attended my training sessions and who always offer great insights into what works in the classroom. Finally, thanks to Gordon at Kall Kwik for his design work and to Alison and Andy Metcalfe for providing a space in which to write.

Table of Contents

Introduction 14

Defining Outstanding 16

Why does outstanding matter to you? 18

Outstanding Teaching as Habit Cultivation 20

Marking for Progress 22

Formative Feedback 23

Implementing Targets 24

Tracking Targets 26

Making Targets Personal and Relevant 27

Using Marking to Plan, Challenge and Intervene 29

Modelling and Scaffolding Targets 31

Understanding What Progress Looks Like 32

Framing the Lesson with a Question 34

Starting with the End in Mind 35

Diagnostic Questioning 36

Identifying Common Misconceptions 37

Circulating Effectively 38

Verbal Feedback 40

The Key Features of Highly Effective Feedback 42

Thinking Time 44

Rephrasing Questions 46

Planning Questions	48
Considering the Aim and Purpose of Questions	50
Facilitating Quality Discussion	51
Signposting	52
Making Success Criteria Matter	54
Adapting Success Criteria	56
Purposeful Activities	57
Bloom's Based Activities	58
Challenge Within Activities	59
Targeted Practice	60
Defining and Directing Effort	62
Training Students	63
Activity Training	64
System Training	65
Thinking Training	66
Visualising Progress	67
Personalising Scaffolding	69
Normalise Mistakes	70
Modelling	71
Modelling Thinking	73
Modelling Questioning	75
Exemplar Work	77
Ownership	78

Pay Attention to the Whole Class 79

Effective Mid-Lesson Reviews 80

Introduce, Observe, Intervene 82

Clarity 83

Tying Homework to Subsequent Lessons 84

Every Second Counts 85

Save Your Energy 86

A Brief Request 88

Introduction

Going from good to outstanding means different things for different people. For some, it is about developing their skills as a teacher. For others, it is about maximising the progress of the pupils in their class. While for others, it is about demonstrating to senior colleagues your ability to teach lessons from the very top drawer.

Often, it's about all three of these things – and more as well.

Whatever you reason for wanting to move from good to outstanding, this book aims to help you on your way. It doesn't offer any guarantees – but it does give you a whole host of strategies, activities and techniques you can employ to take your teaching to the next level.

The ideas are mapped against the principles underpinning commonly-agreed performance criteria for outstanding teaching. They're not about ticking boxes, but about doing things which have a real impact in the classroom. And, ultimately, that is what going from good to outstanding is all about: increasing your impact, so that more learning is happening and students are getting more out of your lessons as a result.

So read on and enjoy – and good luck in your efforts to teach outstanding lessons. I'm certain you'll do a great job.

Defining Outstanding

01 There is always a subjective element to any judgement regarding teacher quality – particularly if that judgement concerns an individual lesson. With that said, a clear set of criteria provide an objective counterweight, albeit one which still has to be interpreted by the observer.

This leads us to why it is important to define what outstanding means in our context.

If you wish to move from good to outstanding in terms of the judgements others are making about your teaching, then you need to have a clear, unambiguous understanding of what they class as outstanding teaching. Their definition becomes your definition.

If, on the other hand, you want to move from good to outstanding in your own eyes, then you need to sit down and spend five minutes defining what outstanding means to you, as well as how this differs from good.

In both cases, it is about you gaining a clear insight into what you are aiming for – whether that is decided internally, by you, or externally, by someone else.

From my own perspective, I would describe outstanding teaching as teaching which maximises progress; caters to the needs of all students; sets and maintains a high level of challenge; is built upon high expectations, strong subject knowledge and sound pedagogy; and cultivates a positive, learning-focussed atmosphere in which effort, persistence and good humour are prized as virtues.

This is the definition I will use to underpin the remainder of the book.

Why does outstanding matter to you?

02 This is your second task: working out why being outstanding matters to you. If you have a clear sense of why you want to be outstanding, then it becomes easier to match your actions and decisions to this deeper purpose.

It is worth considering the point for a few minutes. After all, some teachers may say they want to move from good to outstanding simply as a platitude. Or, they may say it because they think it is the right thing to say.

I imagine your reasoning runs deeper than this and may include one of the following:

- It matters because you want your students to do as well as they can, and you believe outstanding lessons will help achieve this.

- It matters because you are ambitious and you want others to see that you are capable of improving the quality of your teaching until it hits the very highest standards.

- It matters because you think developing yourself professionally is the right thing to do – for your students, yourself and the school you work in.

Whatever your answer to the question 'Why does outstanding matter to me?' once you have your answer in place you have a defined purpose animating your actions. Something you can use to make decisions, and something on which you can fall back if you don't succeed as quickly as you hope.

Outstanding Teaching as Habit Cultivation

03 One way to think about outstanding teaching is as habit cultivation. What distinguishes good teachers from outstanding teachers? Outstanding teachers have developed more habits which help them to be outstanding.

For example, a good teacher might give formative feedback regularly, while only providing students with implementation time on an intermittent basis. An outstanding teacher would give regular formative feedback and maintain **the habit of following this up with dedicated implementation time.**

In another example, a good teacher might regularly check understanding during the course of the lesson, but not always act on this by adjusting and adapting the activities. An outstanding teaching would regularly check understanding and be in **the habit of always using the information they elicit to reshape the lesson on the hoof.**

In these examples we can see that outstanding teaching is often about taking what you know is great practice and making a conscious effort to ensure it becomes a habitual part of your teaching – rather than something you do on some occasions, but not others.

As we continue through the book, consider how you could turn some (or all!) of the ideas which follow into habits you consistently pursue in your teaching, planning and marking.

Marking for Progress

04 We all mark, but the efficacy of that marking is usually higher among outstanding teachers. Marking for progress means setting out with the intention that your marking will make a significant contribution to the progress students make in the lessons to come. Here are some examples of what that might look like:

- Timing when you mark books so that the lesson in which students receive their feedback contains multiple opportunities for them to put it into practice.
- Marking so that students are expected to do something in response. For example, by posing a question or by asking them to identify the errors in their work. This needs to be followed up by dedicated lesson time in which students can respond.
- Marking in advance of formal assessments so that students can apply the information your marking provides when completing these.
- On some occasions, marking in the evening so students can use your feedback the next day.
- Timing your marking so you can use the information you elicit to adapt and amend the next lesson, or even a whole sequence of lessons.

Formative Feedback

05 It goes without saying that formative feedback is a hallmark of outstanding teaching. That is, feedback which contains rich information students can use to make progress.

You might like to think of feedback as a window into your expertise. Remember, you are the expert in the classroom – in terms of subject knowledge, understanding how to think effectively, general cultural knowledge and knowledge about skills and techniques.

When you give feedback, you give students access to this expertise.

Outstanding teachers do this regularly, providing formative feedback verbally and in writing. They may do the former dozens of times in a lesson.

During activities, circulate through the class and observe what students are doing. Look for opportunities to provide feedback which gives students access to your expertise. This will help them to work more effectively. Having given the feedback, leave students and then return later to see whether they have made good use of it. This second part is crucial to ensuring your feedback is put into action.

Implementing Targets

06 Up and down the country many good teachers give their students acres and acres of outstanding feedback. So why are these teachers not yet outstanding?

Because they don't ensure that their students have dedicated lesson time in which to work on implementing their targets.

Feedback is loop, and you need to close that loop. First we give feedback, then the student takes on board that feedback, then they implement the feedback, then we analyse their work and provide new feedback.

You should plan dedicated lesson time in which the focus is on target implementation. Here are three examples:

- Set aside twenty minutes at the start of every third lesson. During this time students' focus is exclusively on trying to implement their targets.

- When setting students an extended piece of work, ask them to write their target at the top of the page (or to remind themselves of this if it is a practical subject). Then, ask them to focus on putting their target into practice while they complete their work.

- Set homework in which students have to redo a piece of work, based on their most recent target. Follow this up in the starter activity of the next lesson.

Tracking Targets

07 It is easy for formative targets to get lost. Verbal feedback disappears into the ether. Written targets can disappear into books or on pieces of paper filed away for safe-keeping.

Tracking targets means collecting formative feedback in one place, so you and your students can easily refer to it. This makes implementing the feedback simpler. It also makes assessing student progress easier when marking their work.

Avoid trying to record and track verbal feedback. It is unmanageable and quickly becomes self-defeating. However, you can track written targets by:

- Sticking a sheet in the front of students' books where these targets are recorded.

- Asking students to transfer the key messages from your written feedback to the inside cover of their exercise books, along with the date when it was given.

- Setting up a spreadsheet in which you make a brief note (one or two words will do) of what each student should be focussing on at present. This can be a supplement to the spreadsheet you use to track students' summative grades.

Making Targets Personal and Relevant

08 Students are more likely to attend to their targets if they feel they are personal and relevant. Such targets are intrinsically more meaningful. If something is meaningful, we are more inclined to pursue it or to alter our behaviour so that it marries up with the thing in question.

You can make targets personal and relevant in the following ways:

- Use the student's name when giving a target.

- Ensure the target accurately reflects the work students have produced. You can emphasise this fact by drawing attention to something specific the student has done which connects to the target you have set them.

- When students receive their marked work, circulate through the room and speak to individual students about their targets. Tell them why you gave that particular target and how you think it will benefit them.

- When getting students to implement their targets (see Entry Six) explain in advance why this is relevant to them. Couch this in terms of the enhanced skills/knowledge/ability they will possess when they have successfully implemented their targets.

- If you have time, speak to students one-to-one about their targets. Talk them through what their target means, why it's important and how they can use it. If appropriate, model target implementation for them.

Using Marking to Plan, Challenge and Intervene

09 When you mark you gain access to a huge amount of information about what students know, what they understand and what they can do. You can use this information to inform your planning, to inform how you challenge students, and to inform the interventions you make. Here's how:

Planning

- If similar mistakes or misconceptions keep cropping up, rejig the starter of your next lesson so as to teach away from these.

- If most students are getting everything right, revisit your planning to see whether you can skip ahead or introduce more challenging content.

Challenge

- Pose students challenging questions in response to pieces of work you mark. Give them time in the next lesson to respond to these.

- As you mark, make a note of who is getting onto the extension questions. Aim to push these students further in the next lesson – and to chivvy along those who are not currently getting to the extensions.

Interventions

- When marking a set of books, start out with the intention of identifying the five students who would most benefit from sustained support in the following lesson.

- As you mark, record summative grades in a spreadsheet. Use this to identify underperforming individuals and groups and to plan relevant interventions.

Modelling and Scaffolding Targets

10 Some students struggle to use the targets they are given. This is often because they do not understand the target or how to implement it.

Outstanding teachers tend to be aware of this possibility. They observe how each student in the class responds to their targets during dedicated implementation time. If a student appears to be struggling, they step in.

Modelling a target gives a student a way through which to understand it. For example, an English teacher who has set a student the target of including more analytical detail in their work may sit down and model what this means by giving three or four examples. Through this, they open up the target for their student, providing context and exemplification which helps the student to make sense of it.

Scaffolding a target means breaking it down or doing a little of the work for the student. This makes it easier for them to access the target and may also free up some of their working memory. For example, a PE teacher who has set a student the target of finishing their javelin throw in a more stable position might break this down into three steps: run-up, mid-throw, and release.

Understanding What Progress Looks Like

11 Often, outstanding teaching is judged in terms of how much progress has been made by all students in a class. Understanding what progress looks like means being able to accurately judge whether you are doing enough of the right things to secure great learning gains across the board.

Progress differs from subject to subject and between age groups. However, all progress is linked by the common fact that it entails students being able to do more or know more than was previously the case. Applying this definition to the subject and/or age-group you teach means having an unambiguous way through which to judge progress.

For example, an A Level Economics teacher may take the definition and connect it to their subject and age group. This leads them to an understanding that, in most lesson, progress means students being able to articulate an enhanced knowledge and understanding of key economic ideas and being able to apply these with greater skill than before the lesson began.

Whereas, a Year 4 teacher delivering a Geography lesson may take the definition and use it to understand that progress means students being able to demonstrate much improved map skills at the end of a fifty minute session.

In short, understanding what progress looks like makes it easier to plan and teach lessons in which outstanding progress is the norm.

Lesson with a Question

...iving the lesson a title, give it a ... or example, 'Comparing worship in Judaism and Hinduism' becomes 'How similar are Jewish and Hindu worship?'

This has a number of benefits which can help you to deliver an outstanding lesson.

First, questions are directional. They provide a goal to which you and the class can direct your behaviour. That goal is trying to find an answer to the question. This automatically gives your lesson a sense of enquiry – something which a standard title does not.

Second, you can return to the question during the lesson and ask students to assess their current progress against it. This involves them judging how well they can now answer the question and what they still need to find out to develop their answers.

Third, you can use the question to assess progress when you are circulating and working with groups or individuals. For example, the RS teacher in our example may set up a main activity in which students are working in pairs to analyse key sources. While this is going on, she could pose the lesson question to a number of pairs, judging their progress (and whether to intervene) as she goes.

Starting with the End in Mind

13 One way to make planning outstanding lessons easier is to start with the end in mind. By this I don't mean the plenary. Instead, I'm talking about the endpoint you want your students to reach. How far do you want them to have travelled, compared to the beginning of the lesson? What do you want them to be able to do or know, compared to when they enter the room?

Having defined your endpoint, ask yourself whether this level of progress really does represent outstanding. If it does, that's great, you can start planning your lesson. If it doesn't, ask yourself why and then up the ante. This brief evaluation is vital – it makes you pay close attention to what you think outstanding progress looks like, compelling you to make changes early on if you decide you've fallen a little short.

Many teachers who struggle to move from good to outstanding stymie their chances by unwittingly planning lessons in which it is only possible for students to make good progress. Avoid falling into this trap by starting with the end in mind.

Diagnostic Questioning

Diagnostic questioning is any questioning which allows you to diagnose the current state of student knowledge and understanding. It's so-called because once you have asked these questions you are in a position to diagnose the student's current position and to make a prescription for change. That prescription comes in the form of changes to the lesson, advice, feedback, guidance, or further questioning.

Asking questions with the intention of diagnosing where students are currently at – or what they are struggling with – means eliciting information which you can use to tailor your teaching so that it meets the needs of your students. This is what outstanding teachers do.

A good tip is to regularly circulate through the classroom, honing in on key students whose knowledge and understanding you want to know more about. Another option is to use whole-class feedback (WCF) techniques. This sees you asking diagnostic questions to the whole class and using the information to tailor what happens next. Visit my website www.mikegershon.com for a free resource containing 25 WCF techniques (The Whole-Class Feedback Guide).

Identifying Common Misconceptions

15 Each area of the curriculum has common misconceptions connected to it. These are those misconceptions which arise again and again, year after year. For example:

- That all metals are magnetic
- That evaluation means saying whether you like something or not
- That 40 + 4 = 404
- That monkeys will evolve into humans
- That poems have to rhyme

Identifying common misconceptions in advanced means you are in a position to teach away from these in your lessons. This is a feature of outstanding teaching. The teacher predicts where students will make mistakes, draws these mistakes out and then uses them as a teaching point.

One option is to use common misconceptions as the basis of a starter activity. Display one on the board, along with a statement such as: 'This is a common mistake many students make in this topic. Why is it a mistake and why do you think students make it?'

This provokes a rich discussion in which students immediately begin analysing and dispelling a common misconception you have identified.

Circulating Effectively

16 I've mentioned circulating a few times already. This is when we leave the front and move around the class. We circulate through the room with the intention of working with different students.

To circulate more effectively – to make your circulating really count – try the following strategies:

- Before you set off, identify the three key students you want to talk to. Consider why you want to talk to them and what impact your intervention should have.

- Think of the two key questions you want to ask students. These questions should be ones that will push their learning on and make them think.

- Identify who is finding the work difficult. Make a beeline for these students and use scaffolding and/or modelling to help them.

- Pick out two or three more-able students for whom the work will be fairly straightforward. Go to these students first and make things harder for them by posing an additional question or by providing an additional success criterion.

- Set out with the intention of eliciting as much information about student learning as possible – through listening, observing and by asking questions.

Verbal Feedback

17 Verbal feedback gives students access to your expertise in the moment. They can use this feedback to adapt and alter what they are doing. Outstanding teachers tend to find lots of opportunities to deliver verbal feedback while they are teaching. For example:

- During activities they circulate, giving students feedback, advice or asking them questions as they go.

- During individual tasks, such as independent writing, they identify specific students to talk to. During these discussions they provide feedback and guidance.

- During group work, they invite groups up to the front of the class in turn. The groups tell them about their work and the teacher responds with verbal feedback. The groups can then use this to improve their work.

- When students make mistakes, the teacher steps in and talks to them about these mistakes. Through their feedback they either help students to work out what they've done wrong, or provide guidance which will send them in the right direction.

- When students answer a question, the teacher uses this as an opportunity to give feedback in response. For example, they suggest another area the student might think about, or encourage them to go away and develop their answer in a certain direction.

The Key Features of Highly Effective Feedback

18 Some pieces of feedback are more effective than others. We've already noted (Entry Six) that students need implementation time if they are to make best use of your feedback. Here we can provide a handy checklist of the key features of highly effective feedback:

- It is personalised;

- It indicates what the student has done well;

- It gives **one** target;

- If necessary, it explains what the student needs to do to implement the target;

- It is clear and unambiguous.

This checklist applies to written feedback and verbal feedback. In the case of the latter, it can be tweaked to take account of the different nature of the student-teacher interaction (spoken, rather than written). As an added bonus, here's a checklist of how to give your feedback a growth mindset focus:

- Focuses on processes, not products;

- Helps students to target their efforts;

- Encourages students to embrace challenges;

- May cause students to reflect on their thinking;

- Is underpinned by the belief the student can develop their intelligence/skill/ability regardless of who they are.

Outstanding teachers ensure their feedback consistently fits with one or both of these checklists.

Thinking Time

19 Often, good teachers and outstanding teachers ask the same questions.

Outstanding teachers tend always to give students thinking tine, though. Whereas good teachers may only do this on occasion, or even not at all.

Thinking time is important. It provides the space in which students can process the information contained in and connected to your questions. They need this space to be able to come up with a high-quality answer.

If you ask questions and expect immediate responses, chances are those responses will be variable in their quality – and often at the lower end of the spectrum. You can provide thinking time in the following ways:

- Pose a question and then wait before taking any answers.

- Pose a question and then say 'Thirty seconds silent thinking, then we'll hear some ideas.'

- Pose a question and then invite students to discuss their thoughts with a partner before taking any answers.

- Pose a question and invite students to first spend 20-30 seconds noting down their thoughts.

- Pose a question and invite students to discuss their thoughts with three other people before getting ready to share them with the class as a whole.

Rephrasing Questions

20 As has been implicit in a number of the entries thus far, outstanding teachers are constantly alive to the needs of their class. They elicit information about student learning – through marking, observation, listening and questioning – and use this information to shape their teaching so it is tailored to meet the needs of their learners.

When it comes to questions, outstanding teachers continue along this path.

Whenever they pose a question – whether to an individual, a pair, a group or the whole class – they observe what impact this has. And, if necessary, they rephrase the question. Sometimes they even rephrase it a number of times, until it works for their students.

For example, an outstanding GCSE English teacher might go through the following rephrasing:

- Do you agree that the poem is a meditation on the transience of life?

- Do you think the poem is actually about the fact that life doesn't last forever?

- What lines in the poem make you think about the passage of time?

Here we see the teacher gradually simplifying their questions until they reach a point at which students can comfortably answer. Having found this point, they might then work back up to the initial question.

Planning Questions

21 Not all questions need to be planned. It is perfectly possible to come up with great questions on the hoof. In fact, sometimes the best questions are spontaneous – prompted by the trains of thought to which our lessons give rise.

If you want to move from good to outstanding though, it can be helpful to plan some of your questions in advance. This is particularly true if questioning is an area on which you find yourself falling down.

Planning questions can involve:

- Identifying one really challenging question for each section of your lesson – something that will make students think differently.

- Identifying 'stingray' style questions relevant to the topic. These are questions which pack a jolt and turn students' thinking on its head.

- Developing a series of questions you can use to push students' thinking by asking one after the other.

- Planning specific questions for specific groups of students. For example, you might plan nine differentiated questions for your main lesson activity, with these divided into three groups of three.

- Planning specific questions for specific students. For example, planning higher-level questions for a more-able student.

Considering the Aim and Purpose of Questions

22 How often do you consider the aim and/or purpose of your questions before you pose them? Good teachers tend to think about this inconsistently, whereas outstanding teachers tend to keep it at the forefront of their minds.

If you have a clear sense of what you are trying to do with your questions, then it is likely the questions you ask will be of a higher standard, that they will link more closely to your students' needs, and that they will lead to greater progress.

To help you on your way, here is a non-definitive list of aims and purposes which can underpin questions:

- To check knowledge or understanding
- To problematize existing knowledge
- To redirect student thinking
- To make a student think about something from a different perspective
- To challenge student thinking
- To elicit justification
- To probe for misconceptions
- To draw out and teach away from mistakes
- To encourage reflection

Facilitating Quality Discussion

23 Discussion features regularly in outstanding lessons. It gives students a chance to articulate their thoughts, gain access to the thoughts of others, and to refine and develop their thinking. It also helps to break up the cognitive load. For example, if you ask students to discuss a key idea first, then write about it, you ensure they can attend to each process separately, with their full working memory.

Facilitating quality discussion means paying attention to a few factors:

- The quality of the questions or stimulus material

- The established classroom norms governing how students interact during discussions

- The scaffolding which might be necessary to support student discussion – for example: sub-questions, keywords displayed on the board, support materials on tables

- Your role in the room – including whether you intervene or take a back seat

- The timescale, including whether you divide the discussion up – for example, you might present students with three connected questions and give them 90 seconds to discuss each one

Signposting

Signposts tell us what is coming up ahead, further down the line.

In outstanding lessons, signposting means telling students what is coming up, further into the lesson.

Why does this matter?

If students know what to expect, they can prepare for it. If they know what is coming up, they know what they are working towards. This is motivational. If students know where the lesson is heading, they can use this information to make sense of what you are asking them to do now, in the present.

These three points illustrate why signposting helps motivate students and secure greater progress.

Here are three simple signposting techniques:

- At the start of the lesson present students with a 'lesson menu' showing them what the starter, main course and dessert (plenary) will look like.

- At the start of the lesson, indicate what the key milestones in the lesson will be. You might even like to make a note of these on the whiteboard. As you hit the milestones, remind students of what they have done so far and of what is coming next.

- Begin the lesson by showing students what they will be able to do at the end. Return to this at key points, giving them a chance on each occasion to consider how close they are to hitting their goal.

Success Criteria Matter

Success criteria ensure students know what they need to be successful. Outstanding teachers make them matter. This means students engage and interact with them, instead of just seeing them as another piece of information displayed on the board – one among many.

You can make success criteria matter in the following ways:

- Develop them in conjunction with your students. This binds them into the process and gives them ownership.

- Give each success criterion a colour. Provide students with pens or pencils of the same colour. Invite students to indicate with an appropriately coloured star each part of their work which connects to each success criterion.

- Print out the success criteria and give students a copy to have on their desks. Circulate during the task and engage students in discussion about the criteria.

- Display a piece of exemplar work and highlight which sections illustrate each of the success criteria. This helps students to visualise what success looks like.

- As students are working, circulate through the room and identify examples of success criteria being met. Praise this, specify why it is good and draw other students' attention to it.

Adapting Success Criteria

At times, the success criteria you give students may be inappropriate. They might be too difficult or too easy. In either case, your estimation of what students can do has been proved wrong by circumstances.

This is fine – it happens to all of us. Getting success criteria right isn't a zero-sum game. It's more about tweaking and adapting in response to the evidence of your lesson.

To go from good to outstanding, ensure that you are ready to adapt your success criteria if the need arises.

If they turn out to be too easy, tell the class you've noticed this and are going to increase the level of challenge as a result. You can do this by adding additional criteria, by making the existing criteria more complex, or by removing a criterion altogether and replacing it with a new, more difficult, one.

If they turn out to be too hard, tell the class you've noticed this and are going to make it a little easier for them to succeed. You can do this by simplifying one or more of the criteria, by removing a criterion, or by breaking the criteria down into separate, smaller sections.

Purposeful Activities

27 Activities with purpose lead to greater progress than activities which appear to lack purpose, or in which purpose is ill-defined. This is because students seek meaning – and if they don't see it, they are likely to become less focussed as a result (questioning why they are being asked to do the particular activity).

To ensure your activities always retain a clear sense of purpose, use the following checklist:

- Does the activity link directly to the LO?
- Is the activity sufficiently challenging that pupils will feel like they are getting something out of it?
- Can I quickly articulate the purpose of the activity in a short sentence?

If you answer 'yes' to these three questions then your activity should be fine. If you answer 'no' to any of them, then you may need to look again.

On looking again, consider the activity from the student's point of view. What will they be thinking and feeling as they try to do what you are asking them to do? Will it make sense to them? Will they immediately intuit the purpose behind what they are doing?

Bloom's Based Activities

28 Bloom's Taxonomy of Educational Objectives is the outstanding teacher's friend. It provides a ready-made structure for lessons and activities which ensures an increasing degree of challenge and allows you to tailor what you plan to the needs of your students. For practical students there is also a useful but less well known Taxonomy of the Psycho-Motor Domain.

Planning activities based on Bloom's taxonomy means almost guaranteeing excellent progress in your lesson. Here are three techniques to try:

- Plan the lesson as whole so it moves up the taxonomy. Start with a knowledge/comprehension task, move onto an application/analysis activity, and then finish with an evaluation/synthesis task.

- Plan an individual activity containing three parts. Part one should be knowledge/comprehension; part two application/analysis; and part three evaluation/synthesis.

- Plan extension questions for all activities based on the categories of analysis, evaluation and synthesis.

(Visit www.mikegershon.com for my free Bloom's Taxonomy resource, The Bloom Buster.)

Challenge Within Activities

29 Maintaining a high degree of challenge within individual activities is crucial if you want to sustain outstanding progress across a lesson. A common pitfall among teachers trying to get from good to outstanding is that only some lesson activities are sufficiently challenging. For example, they may have a starter and first activity which are relatively easy, followed by challenging second and third activities.

Here are three ways to ensure the level of challenge remains high within all your activities:

- Use Bloom's Taxonomy to structure the activity or as the basis for extension questions or tasks.

- Divide activities in two. Make the first part of the activity the standard element, which will challenge some students but not all. Make the second part of the activity the additional element, which will challenge every student (although it is likely only some of the class will get onto this part).

- Create a box of challenging questions connected to your subject or which are relevant for your age group. If any student finishes an activity sooner than you expect (a signal that it is not sufficiently challenging), bring out the box and let them choose a challenge question to think about.

Targeted Practice

30 Practice makes perfect. Repetition plays a significant role in learning of all kinds.

The most effective practice is practice which is targeted. That means the student is trying to do something specific as part of their practice. They are attending to the task in hand with their full working memory.

As examples, consider a footballer who practices free kicks by draping a flag from the crossbar and trying to hit this. Or a cellist who practise a piece of music by first focussing relentlessly on the most complex sections.

You can include targeted practice in your lessons with the following techniques:

- By providing students with a variety of different questions connected to the topic, which they have to answer by applying the same skill in different ways. This is most easily seen in Maths.

- By telling individual students what you want them to focus on while they are practising. For example, a Year 3 teacher might tell a student to really focus on the shape of their vowels while they are practising handwriting.

- By giving students a specific target to aim at. For example, a PE teacher might tell badminton students that they need to able to hit a shuttlecock to within six inches of the back of the court, three times in a row.

Defining and Directing Effort

31 In the last entry we considered the importance of targeted practice. In such situations, student effort is directed at the teacher's behest – either through the activity structure or through the instructions the teacher gives.

Defining and directing effort is, in general, a common feature of outstanding teaching. This is because it enables students to first understand what effort is, and then how that effort ought to be used to achieve greatest success.

When defining effort, it is important to give students concrete examples of what good effort means to you. The term on its own is broad, potentially vague and easily corrupted into an empty platitude. Showing students pieces of work which are the result of high levels of effort, or defining what effort will look like in a specific task, means students have something tangible to think about.

Directing effort is then much easier. If students know what good effort looks like, they have a clear sense of what they should do to direct their own efforts. You can further support them by circulating during activities and specifying what you would like to see from different individuals in terms of their effort.

Training Students

32 Training students means teaching them routines and systems. When they have mastered these, they no longer need to think actively about them. Working memory is freed up for thinking about the lesson. The routines and systems become second nature.

For example, an outstanding Year 6 teacher might start the year by training their students in:

- How to enter the room
- How to give out books
- How to tidy up at the end of lessons and at the end of the day
- How to discuss in pairs and in groups
- How to ask for help
- How to use trial and error
- How to use mistakes as a learning opportunity

By dedicating some curriculum time to this at the start of the year, the teacher frees up a huge amount of time (cumulatively) over the rest of the year. Students can fall back on their training again and again. They don't need to think about what to do in the situations outlined above. Instead, they just get on and do what the teacher has trained them to do.

Activity Training

33 We'll now look at three specific examples of training, the first of which is activity training. Every teacher uses certain activity types over and again. For example: paired discussion, group work, team games, independent writing.

And most teachers have a subset of specific activities they like to return to. Mine include: silent debate, speed debating, stepped questions, evaluation tables.

Training students in the activities you commonly use means training them in how to do those activities. This means students become more adept at engaging with the lesson content you use those activities to teach.

For example, imagine a class who have been trained how to use paired discussion effectively. Every time the teacher includes such an activity in a lesson, those students will immediately know what to do – and how to do it most successfully.

This means no time is lost to students working out what they need to do. Over the course of a year significant gains are made through the accumulation of marginal gains every time the teacher uses the given activity.

System Training

34 Our second training example is system training.

Systems are those procedures you have in place in your classroom for getting certain things done. They can be practical, such as:

- A system for moving the tables
- A system for checking the room at the end of the day
- A system for returning work when it has been marked

Or they can be connected to learning, such as:

- A system for peer- and self-assessment (e.g. green pen; two stars and a wish; even better if)
- A system for tackling problems (e.g. three before me)
- A system for analysing sources (e.g. RAVEN, the critical thinking acronym)

Training students in systems means providing ways of operating on which they can continually rely. This makes it easier for them to be successful in your classroom. It also frees you up to focus on tailoring your interventions so they best support the needs of the students in front of you.

Thinking Training

35 Our third training example is thinking training. Here, we are concerned with training students in how to think in specific situations. For example:

- Head up, look for space, move or play the ball: a thinking technique a PE teacher might use.

- Point, Evidence, Explain, Link (PEEL): a thinking technique an English teacher might teach his students for writing paragraphs.

- Measure twice, cut once: a thinking technique a DT teacher might train her woodwork class to use.

- Write your ideas on scrap paper, look at them, edit them, decide how to start: a thinking technique a Year 5 teacher might train their students to use before beginning a piece of writing.

In each case, the training gives the students in question a tool on which they can repeatedly call. This makes it easier for them to think and work successfully. It also means the teacher can remind them of the training if they forget or become stuck. Finally, by training students how to think, the teacher can be sure that everybody in the class has something on which they can fall back, helping to create a group of independent learners.

Visualising Progress

36 Some students struggle to remain motivated. Often, these learners lack faith in their own abilities. They do not believe that they can make progress. They also find it difficult to accept or understand the progress they have already made.

Outstanding teachers are usually good at helping these learners to visualise the progress they've made. This gives them a tangible sense of where they are now, compared to where they were. Through this, they gain a sense of motivation and purpose, making it easier for them to start believing in themselves. Here are three simple ways to visualise progress for your students:

- Record targets at the front of their books (see Entry Seven). Sign these off when students achieve them. You can then point to this as evidence of the progress learners have made.

- Take a couple of minutes to flick through the student's book with them. Take them back to the start of the year and highlight the differences between their work now and their work then. Tie this change to their actions and efforts.

- Ask students to show you or tell you about something they've mastered since the start of the year. Ask them why they now find this easy. Highlight that this progress is a result of the decisions they've made and the things they've done in lessons.

Personalising Scaffolding

37 Scaffolding is anything we do which makes it a little easier for students to access a task. For example:

- Sentence starters
- Suggesting a possible answer which you and the student then discuss
- A writing frame
- Simplifying the task
- Breaking down a big question into three sub-questions

Personalising scaffolding involves:

1) Identifying those students most in need of your support.

2) Working with them one-on-one or in a small group.

3) Giving them personalised support and guidance based on what they are struggling to do.

For example, a good teacher might provide sentence starters for the whole class to use. Whereas an outstanding teacher would do this, then work with the three students who were still struggling – giving them examples of how to turn the sentence starters into their opening sentences.

Normalise Mistakes

38 In outstanding classrooms mistakes are welcomed. They are seen as learning opportunities. The teacher makes a conscious effort to use them as teaching points. They talk about 'good mistakes' and 'teaching away from mistakes'. They thank students for making 'good mistakes', using this as an opportunity to help the whole class better understand key ideas.

They might also collate mistakes and misconceptions and use these as the basis of activities (see Entry Fifteen). And they are likely to have clearly defined responses ready-to-go if any student seeks to undermine a peer who has made a mistake:

- Danny, that isn't how we work in this class. Apologise to Charlotte for what you said about her mistake, please. Mistakes are good because they help us to learn. Everybody should be free to make them – I want to see mistakes, because then I know you're being challenged to think really carefully.

Finally, these teachers will encourage the use of trial and error (which they might call trial and improvement) and diminish the costs of failure by making clear that failures are events from which we can learn, not marks of who we are.

Modelling

39 In the Sutton Trust's report of October 2014 'What makes great teaching?' teacher modelling was highlighted as a consistent feature of outstanding teaching, across a range of different education systems.

Modelling is anything you do which shows students how to do something, how to think, or what something means. It is about opening up knowledge and understanding, communicating key information to students in the process.

Outstanding teachers model throughout their lessons. This includes:

- Modelling thinking. For example, by narrating how they might approach a problem or by explaining the different ways a piece of work could be tackled.

- Modelling activities. For example, by showing students how to complete an activity or by demonstrating what each stage of an activity will entail.

- Modelling ideas. For example, by demonstrating what an idea looks like in practice, or by showing images which are representative of an idea outside the classroom.

- Modelling processes. For example, by walking students through how to set up a science experiment, or by demonstrating how to translate a design into a 3D model.

Modelling Thinking

40 Let us think about modelling thinking a little further.

You are an expert in thinking. You know how to think about the subject or topic you are teaching. You also know how you want your students to think. For example, a History teacher wants their students to think critically about sources, to think analytically about essay writing and to think astutely about interpretations of historical events.

By modelling how to think in different situations, you give students access to your expertise.

They can then imitate this, which is the first step on the road to internalising it and being able to think that way themselves, without the need for support.

Here are five simple ways to model thinking:

- Annotate a question, activity or exam script with the thinking you would do if faced with it.

- Create an exemplar piece of work. Annotate this with the thinking which underpins each element.

- At the start of an activity, take students through two or three examples of how to tackle the task. For each one, talk through your thinking.

- If a student is stuck, ask them to talk you through their thinking. Armed with this information you can then model how they could think differently and, therefore, overcome the problem.

- Draw a diagram showing how to think about a particular problem. For example, a simple flow-chart. Leave this on the board so students can refer to it while they work.

Modelling Questioning

41 Outstanding learners usually ask questions. Specifically, they ask questions which help themselves to learn more and to learn better. For example:

- 'Miss, what would happen if a neutron star was sucked into a black hole?'

- 'Sir, is it possible Shakespeare intended King Lear to be interpreted differently by audiences of the time, compared to how we interpret him today?'

- (to self) 'Now, what made it turn out like that? Did I use too much iodine? Let me check.'

- (to self) 'What was that rule again? Oh yes, I remember. How can I use it with this question?'

By modelling questioning of this type, you can encourage more of your students to pose questions that push their own thinking.

For example, you might work one-on-one with a student, demonstrating some of the questions they could ask about a certain activity. Or, you might display some key questions on the board that students could ask themselves as they read through a specific text.

The key message here is that we are giving students a way to take control of their thinking and their learning. A way through which they can improve both and learn more as a result.

Exemplar Work

42 Outstanding lessons regularly feature exemplar work. This might be on the walls as part of a display. It might form part of an 'exemplar work booklet' the teacher makes for their students. Or it might be that the teacher talks students through individual pieces of exemplar work relevant to certain activities.

Exemplar work provides learners with a great insight into what they need to do to be successful. It shows them what high quality work looks like, giving them a starting point for creating their own.

Making consistent use of exemplar work will help you to teach outstanding lessons. Here are some further examples of what to do:

- Create a bank of exemplar work by collecting, photocopying (and possibly anonymising) great pieces of work students produce.
- Create exemplar work yourself prior to or during the lesson. In the latter case, it can sometimes be fun to create your work at the same time as students create theirs.
- For practical subjects, use videos or manufactured objects (in DT) as exemplar materials. YouTube is an excellent source of material.

Ownership

43 If students feel ownership over their work, they are more likely to pay it a high level of attention, to work hard over an extended period of time, and to believe that their own efforts are the crucial factor in whether or not they are successful.

Here are three ways to help create a sense of ownership in your lessons:

- Involve students in decision-making processes. For example, how long to spend on an activity, what the success criteria should be and what a high level of effort will look like.

- Praise students for the way in which their efforts have led them to create work of a high standard – instead of just praising the work itself. For example: Rima, the way in which you kept going and tried different techniques to solve the problem has helped you to create an effective report. (Note how the student's actions are tied to the outcome – this sends the message that they have ownership over their work).

- Give students options and choices. For example, set up an activity and give students three choices about how they respond to it. This creates a sense of agency, which in turn lends a feeling of ownership.

Pay Attention to the Whole Class

44 In good lessons, most of the class remain focussed and on task for most of the time. In outstanding lessons, all of the class remain focussed and on task for all of the time.

The best way to achieve this ideal situation is by paying attention to the whole class throughout the lesson. But what does this mean?

In any lesson, there will be times when the teacher's attention is drawn to specific individuals, groups or to procedural matters such as what is happening next or the distribution of resources. These are key points at which you can fail to pay attention to the whole class. If you do this, some students may take it as an opportunity to go off task or stop working.

To overcome the problem, ensure you always position yourself so that you can see – and keep an eye on – everybody in the room. For example, if you are working with a pair of students, try to avoid turning your back on the rest of the room. Instead, talk to them while facing the class – this allows you to keep one eye on everybody else, while you give the pair in question tailored support.

Mid-Lesson Reviews

Mid-lesson reviews are a helpful way to check progress and to remind students of what you and they are trying to achieve. For these reasons they are often found in outstanding lessons.

Stopping the lesson halfway through and taking two minutes to review what has happened, as well as what is coming next, means giving students a moment to reflect on their learning and to recalibrate themselves for the remainder of the session.

Here are five tips for making mid-lesson reviews effective:

- Remind students of the learning objective and ask them to assess how close they are to achieving this.

- Pose a question based on the lesson so far. Ask students to discuss this in pairs before taking answers.

- Display a brief three-point summary of the first half of the lesson. Ask students to predict what will come next, based on this.

- Ask students to reflect on what they have done so far and to identify two questions they want answered in the second half of the lesson.

- In practical lessons, ask students to show their peers what they can do, based on the first half of the lesson. Then ask peers to give feedback on what they've seen.

Introduce, Observe, Intervene

46 This is a technique you can use to maximise the efficacy of your role when presenting students with new ideas or information. It is a simple checklist which summarises the routine most outstanding teachers follow in their classrooms.

First, introduce the new material.

Then, observe student reactions and responses.

Finally, identify whether you need to make a whole-class intervention, or a series of interventions with specific students. Follow through on your decision.

You can turn the three words into a mantra: Introduce, Observe, Intervene. Repeat the mantra to yourself each time you introduce new material. Following the steps religiously means you will always be well-placed to analyse how students are dealing with new content and who will benefit most from your immediate support.

And don't forget that the 'intervene' step can include intervening to make the work more challenging. For example, if you observe that a third of the class have quickly assimilated the new content, then you are in a position to challenge them with a question or follow-up task.

Clarity

47 Good teachers are clear most of the time. In lessons they teach, students generally know what they need to do and why they are doing it.

Outstanding teachers make clarity a virtue. Their students nearly always know what they need to do and why they are doing it. They also know precisely what to do if they are uncertain about something.

Clarity of communication – both written and verbal – minimises the risk of students not knowing what they should be doing. It also minimises the risk of them finding themselves engaged in a task without any real understanding of why they are doing what they've been asked to do.

Increase the clarity of your communication by:

- Using images on slides and handouts to supplement written information.
- Using gestures, body language and physical modelling to supplement verbal information.
- Rehearsing complex explanations in your head before saying them out loud.
- Breaking complex tasks down into a series of separate steps.
- Using students as peer models and re-explainers.

Tying Homework to Subsequent Lessons

48 Demonstrating that the homework you set has a direct impact on the lessons you teach will help to take you from good to outstanding. This signals the extent to which you think carefully about homework, the value you place on it and the relevance it has to the learning you want your students to do.

Setting homework which feeds into your next lesson means ensuring students use time at home to continue making progress. Generic homework activities which fit this approach include:

- Consolidation activities in which students summarise, revisit or reflect on their learning.

- Target-led activities in which students redo, rewrite or revisit work in light of the targets you've set them.

- Research activities in which students research material relevant for the next lesson (and then bring this in with them).

- Reading or video-watching activities in which students assimilate content they can then apply, analyse and evaluate in the following lesson.

- Application activities in which students practice applying what they have learned in the lesson.

Every Second Counts

49 In a good lesson, learning might be happening for 90% of the time. To put it another way, for 90% of the lesson, learning is everybody's number one focus.

In an outstanding lesson, learning will be happening for 99% of the time. For 99% of the lesson, learning will be at the top of everybody's agenda.

That difference, while relatively small, is crucial in maximising student progress. Particularly over the course of a year. If 10% of lesson time does not involve learning and a student has 80 lessons with you over the course of a year (2 per week), then the equivalent of 8 lessons are lost.

To ensure you avoid this situation, work on the basis that every second counts – and communicate this premise to students.

Thinking in this way means you will always be alive to the possibility of your lesson losing focus and of the potential for a lull in effort to creep up out of nowhere (which it can easily do).

Save Your Energy

50 We conclude our journey from good to outstanding with a tip that is often learned the hard way. While planning and marking are important, the single biggest opportunity you have to influence your students – to help them learn – is when you are with them, teaching your lesson.

It follows that this is the point in time when your energy can be best utilised. The return you get, in terms of learning, for each extra bit of energy you put in is higher than at any other time.

This means you need to save your energy.

Sometimes it means spending a little less time on marking and planning. Sometimes it means having a cut-off time in the evenings, beyond which you do no more work. And sometimes it means saying no when somewhere asks you take on extra duties.

Whatever you do to give yourself a break and save your energy, remember that this decision has a direct consequence on student learning, because it determines how much energy you have to spend when you are with your students.

And with that, we draw to a close. Let me finish by wishing you luck in your journey from good to outstanding. You won't be able to implement everything in this book immediately. Pick out two or three strategies and start with those. Turn them into new habits. Then come back and do the same again. Very soon you'll be teaching consistently outstanding lessons; and achieving the goals you've set for yourself.

A Brief Request

If you have found this book useful I would be delighted if you could leave a review on Amazon to let others know.

If you have any thoughts or comments, or if you have an idea for a new book in the series you would like me to write, please don't hesitate to get in touch at mike@mikegershon.com.

Finally, don't forget that you can download all my teaching and learning resources for **FREE** at www.mikegershon.com and www.gershongrowthmindsets.com

Printed in Great Britain
by Amazon